Instagram Marketing:

How to Earn $1000+ Per Month as an Instagram Influencer: How to Grow Your Followers, Increase Your Engagement and Land Paid Sponsorships

Table of Contents

Introduction

Congratulations on purchasing this book and thank you for doing so.

There are several social media platforms and famous influencers that started on each one. We will begin the following chapters discussing the various platforms and trends in today's market and why they are important. Do you know the kind of impact they have on you or the businesses around you? Social media is constantly changing for a better user experience. Both consumers and business are not blind to this and are taking advantage each and every day.

We will dive deep into Instagram, specifically, and cover what exactly it means to be an influencer and how that plays a role in today's economy and social media. Do you know who the hottest influencers currently leading the scene in your favorite industries? How did they get started and what is keeping them afloat? If you are good at what you do or at least have enough people think you are great at what you do, there is certainly money to be had. Being a social media influencer has the potential to be a very lucrative career, and we hope to get you to $1,000 per month after this book! We will give simple tips and trips on the topics everyone wants the secret to:

- How to Grow Your Followers

- How to Increase Your Engagement

- How to Get Paid Sponsorships

There are plenty of books on this subject on the market, thanks again for choosing this one! Every effort was made to ensure it is full of as much useful information as possible, please enjoy!

Chapter 1
Overview of Trends in Social Media

We are all familiar with social media, right? I mean really, how can we not be, but it seems no matter how up to date you might be, social media is an ever-evolving machine. What is current and trending one day may very well be out the next. In order to be successful via social media, you need to always be aware of what's happening, and not only on your favorite platform but across the entire spectrum. That being said, typically you will find that trends spill over from one platform to the next, and quickly. So, what's up and coming - or continuing its popularity reign - this year?

Messaging. In case it was ever a question, millennials preferred method of communication is via messaging which shows prominently through their brand loyalty. Have you noticed the transition from live representatives to automated options? Phone calls or e-mails to chat windows? There's a reason for that. As a whole, we have already started to see a rise in chatbots, and not just in the U.S., but globally. They quickly respond to users' comments and/or questions through artificial intelligence. Want to schedule an appointment with your dentist? Or maybe have a quick question about shipping? There's a bot that can help with that. Think about it. Have you ever wondered how someone responded so quickly to your question? Chances are you are actually speaking with a bot. Chatbots are designed to mimic the typical conversation a human would have and have taken off in providing basic customer service, general inquiries, and/or scheduling. In a Q1 2016 study from sproutsocial.com, those surveyed reported 34.5% prefer their customer care via social media. Facebook Messenger? Hello, chatbots. They are programmed with keywords that allow them to quickly nail down what information it is a consumer is after. Companies like Domino's, CNN, Disney and Whole Foods have all launched their own chatbots to improve customer engagement and satisfaction. Scientists are even making progress in developing an 'emotional' chatbot, which was able to participate in conversation eliciting responses with happiness, sadness, or disgust. Needless to say, they have come leaps and bounds since Microsoft's launch of Tay on Twitter. The bots are now being programmed to look for the keywords that the user provides, but are being taken a step beyond to be able to recognize what emotion is being utilized. Is this consumer happy, mad, or sad? The bots will be able to provide a relevant response to the general information while presenting it in a context that makes sense within the conversation.

The next major trend being seen everywhere are videos. When you think of something going viral, what typically comes to mind? Video. YouTube. Facebook Live. Instagram Stories. Snapchat. And once upon a time, Vine. Yep, you guessed it – millennials want their information, and they want it easily digested. They took home the gold of users that most viewed videos in 2016 and let's be honest, it's doubtful that trend will reverse anytime soon. In 2015, Animoto conducted a survey and found that consumers are four times more likely to watch a video about a product as they are to read about it. In the same survey, they uncovered 84% of consumers admitted they have liked a company video that appeared in their newsfeed. Two months after Instagram launched Instagram Stories, a reported 100 million active users partook. It has also been rumored by 2021 Facebook will be "all video." Doing a live video gives businesses and brands a major edge – it allows them to instantly interact with your target audience and customers in real-time. As we just discussed in messaging, consumers want their information right away. Live video gives consumers the genuine touch they are looking for with immediate satisfaction of having questions or concerns answered. Statistics have shown that a whopping 43% of businesses plan to invest in interactive videos this year alone and in a recent study by Kleiner Perkins, it was estimated 74% of all internet traffic will be represented by video content and, as projected by Cisco, that number will jump to 80% by 2019.

Now let's talk about Augmented Reality. Augmented Reality took off quickly in the U.S., and everyone wants a piece of the pie. Snapchat most certainly blazed the trail starting with static filters before moving on to interactive, but other platforms are not far behind. For instance, the craze of Pokémon Go which was launched in the U.S. on July 6th of 2016. Since that time, it has had over 100 million downloads and over $268 million total revenue. Even if you did not partake in Pokémon Go, chances are pretty high you still have encountered AR. Filters. **Filters**. *Filters*. We have all seen them, and some might be harder to recognize than others (although, the notorious puking of a rainbow or having an adorable cat nose and ears seems pretty realistic to me, right?). This trend is going nowhere. Facebook recently acquired Masquerade, which is a filter app that you can utilize while live streaming. Combining live video *and* filters? Brilliant. Another impressive, and quite successful, use of AR was executed by Rebecca Minkoff through her app Zeekit. Through this app, consumers were able to simply upload a selfie and virtually try on outfits. They are then able to share their photo out on social media to get feedback from friends and family! This trend spread quickly through other markets, noticeably Lowe's launched a Virtual Room Designer, which allows customers to play with the features and design a room utilizing the company's home-improvement products. Users can adjust their perspective to experience the room from different viewpoints (parents or children!). Minkoff and Lowe's took a fun and interactive trend on social media and put a business savvy spin on it to quickly attract the fashion and homemaking market, resulting in the gain of more sales.

Which is a perfect introduction for our next trend: women. A very large majority of top influencers are women, and of those, most are millennials. Now let's go just a tad bit further. A lot of these millennial women are also mothers. According to a study conducted by BabyCenter, 83% of new moms are millennials, and they give birth to about 9,000 babies every single day. These young, new moms are excited to provide their opinions and recommendations. In fact, Forbes reported that 74% of these moms report on average they have 24 close friends in which they share product recommendations amongst. Not only are they excited to share information on different products and brands, but they also have the dollars to back up their purchases. Research conducted by Trybe tells us that these millennial parents have $200 billion in spending power and 85% of these moms are willing to try new products, and easily so. Millennial moms have grown up with the internet, and are seriously plugged in. Whether it's via mobile, laptop or tablet, these moms are active online. Trybe also shared with us another key piece of information – 48% of millennial moms shared that social media was a large influence when they went to purchase a product or service.

As the rise of brands and e-commerce companies in social media grows, so does a number of available business tools. Business users are getting serious about leveraging social media outlets, and it shows not only in their presence but in the strength of tools on the market. If you are new to the platform or social media as a whole, as a consumer or business, it can be a bit overwhelming, but platforms are stepping in to lend a hand. Instagram led the way last year with its launch of an algorithm that would place relevant content in the feed versus the prior method of putting posts in chronological order. As social media continues to refine and finesse their algorithms to make content shown more of what its users want, influencers are becoming more and more popular among businesses. Why? Because people are less likely to watch a :30-second ad when it is very blatantly an ad. YouTube and Snapchat now give users the option to skip an ad, which makes it more difficult for businesses to get their content seen; however, if it is presented in a native matter, it fits more seamlessly into the user's feed. A native ad is a material that is presented in someone else's voice than the actual business or brand promoting their product. For instance, Walmart will run ads on The Bump to target their group expecting mothers. The Bump will create the ad, so it resembles the look and feels of the rest of their content very naturally. Users are more likely to take it as a recommendation from their trusted group of influence or social hero, rather than be turned off by the forcing of products on them. And this is important. Consumers are becoming more and more involved in the buying process. They want to feel empowered in their decision making. When it is presented as a suggestion or recommendation, consumers are more likely to absorb the information being presented to them. Before companies were familiar with this, it was a bit of a struggle which is when native ads took off in popularity. As the economy and trends change, the marketing has no choice but to follow suite if they want to remain afloat. Influencers are rising in popularity and, more times than not, this is a win-win situation for the business and the social start. Tomoson stated, "51% of marketers believe they acquire better customers through influencer marketing". That's a pretty large piece of the puzzle, so that's where you come in.

Influencers get paid through various means to promote a product to encourage the boost of sales for businesses. Brands can promote their product(s) and all the amazing features in all their glory, but if there is no emotional connection with the end-user, there is a less likely chance for purchase. According to mediakix, in 2016 there was more than a 90x increase in influence marketing as compared to 2013. Think back to Chapter 1 where we discussed the rise of chatbots and their progression into being able to grasp the concept of emotion. This is being intertwined in basic customer service so imagine how important the emotional aspect is when it comes to the decision-making process of buying an actual product. Those who are browsing the networks want the reality of an actual person they can genuinely relate to and connect with all while having access to the ease of purchase via social media or online. Studies have shown that as high as 75% of people have admitted that they purchased a product because they saw it on social media. The purchasing channel of social media only falls short to the retailers' website. Social media platforms aren't just at our disposal for fun. After all, they are still businesses and are taking advantage of the times and focusing their efforts on increasing Average Revenue per User (ARPU). As they move towards better user experience, they will, in return, see correlating user value. In July of 2015, eMarketer reported Instagram as the third highest most effective marketing tactic according to U.S. social media users. Sponsored social posts on all platforms beat out the classics: SEO, PPC, and print ads. According to consumers, only televisions ads and sponsored programs could compete with the effectiveness of sponsored social posts. It has been estimated that by the end of the year, Instagram will have gained the remaining large majority of

Snapchat's brands and influencers due to the similar functionalities and superior analysis and measuring tools. So, why does this matter to you? If sponsored posts are resonating and influencing the most with consumers, companies have a need to adjust their tactics accordingly. You don't think influencers became a hot commodity for no reason, do you?

Chapter 2
What's an Influencer?

More and more people, celebrities, and Fortune 500 companies are getting in the game of social media, and 2017 has shown a dramatic shift towards influencer marketing because, if we are being honest, dated techniques don't quite work like they used to. With that being said, there is still one large exception to the rule: word-of-mouth. Influencers are rapidly taking over the scene across all social media channels. If you are even moderately, but actively, engaged on social media, it's likely you want to be one. If you do not want to be one, it is likely you follow one. If you are a brand, it's almost a guarantee you want to have one in your corner. Influencers is an exceptionally fluid term so to put it in very basic terms, they are people who yield influence over others and have established themselves as an individual or team of credible and trusted innovators and leaders in a specific market or niche.

Influencers span multiple categories from food to fashion, tech products to techniques. It could be one specific brand that they are loyal to for everything or one specific product that the only loyalty they have is to the product alone. For example, fitness gurus may swear by Nike products and that alone. From socks to shorts to water bottles: Nike. Maybe you have a serious knack for putting together outfits under $15. From shirts to shoes, to accessories – you have no real brand loyalty, you just like great outfits for even better prices! Or, you could be a food connoisseur, and you want to try every restaurant throughout the U.S. that offers crème brulee. And if not the U.S., then maybe throughout the city you are geographically located in. Whatever your passion may be, the opportunities to share your knowledge or opinions to influence others are endless. See, I told you the term was fluid!

Celebrities were the original form of influencers, but we have seen a large movement towards ordinary (and I use this term very loosely), everyday people who hone in on a particular niche, becoming online "celebrities." Influencer marketing has exploded in recent years opening the market drastically, and for a good reason. Thanks to Digital News Report, we know almost half of online consumers (a massive 47%) use ad blockers because they find them irrelevant or annoying, so research is showing over 50% of companies have a budget solely for sponsored social activity for their brand. Let's take it a step even further with data from eMarketer showing 84% are planning to execute and influencer marketing campaign within the next year.

So now that you have a very brief and shallow overview on why influencers are important, what exactly makes one attractive to a potential sponsor? The first thing is that an influencer embodies the traits and qualities of a brand, making it a natural fit for everyone involved. It creates an easy and effortless flow with the company and consumers due to their following; it's likely their followers are the primary target for the business. For example, a lot of companies have partnered with Latino influencers to gain further reach into the Hispanic market. If a business is trying to break into a new culture that they do not quite grasp, it could be a complete disaster if they do not take the right approach. Utilizing an influencer gives them an edge and peace of mind. The great news is social media is universal, so if you feel confident in multiple cultures, you've already got an edge on most people out there, but for now let's focus on the U.S.

There are a couple different approaches you can take as an influencer. The first is to feature a company's product on your own channel. The alternate is to have them let you perform a one-time takeover on their channel, or have a schedule where you are featured sporadically throughout different periods of the month, quarter or year. An opportune time, for example, would be when a new product is launching. Another time could be if a company has a merge with another or rebranding. Utilizing an influencer not only raises awareness of the news in a positive light, but it also helps build the confidence of consumers in their brand. Being an influencer can be a lot of fun, but we need to remember it is still a job which means there is still a large part that requires business and hard work. You have to invest the time in yourself and in your craft. Would you believe someone's opinion on nuclear science if the first thing they read about it was yesterday? Likely not. Your success won't happen overnight because you put out one great piece of content. You need to be putting out great content every single day. There are a few key items influencers need to encompass and/or keep top of mind for the partnership to make the most sense. These will be important to remember when we get to Chapter 6 and begin to talk about garnering paid sponsorships.

Is there relevance? As discussed in Chapter 1, users are becoming more prone to only view what is relevant to them and block out the rest and, as mentioned before, this was first tapped into through native ads. Companies would partner with brands or other companies to have their ad appear in a very subtle, but effective, manner on their partners' site. This makes it feel like less of an ad and more relevant to the consumer. The internet is overloaded with information, so if the content is not specific and relevant to the consumer, it becomes noise which is ultimately blocked out entirely. Same goes for influencers. If you are not entertaining while remaining relevant, you can consider yourself gone from the view of many. Users act differently dependent upon which channel you utilize, so it is important the conversation you want to have is happening on the channel you want to use as your platform. For example, for Facebook, you would want an entertaining video that is quick and to the point. You wouldn't necessarily spend a lot of time trying to engage with your audience through building a relationship, but instead, focus on gaining their attention as quickly as possible. YouTube, on the other hand, requires a bit more of a connection with your audience through your video thumbnail, video title, and, of course, the actual content contained in the video. Twitter requires little connection per se, but more of a succinct quip to captivate the user's attention. Instagram is king when considering the need to be visually pleasing and interesting.

The next thing to consider is the reach. The reach should be substantial in terms of average users and should provide a greater span than what the business is currently able to do on their own. The reach should also expose the influencer to new potential followers, so there is cross-pollination between the influencer's account the brand's account. Influence is commonly mistaken with the audience, which the two do not always go hand in hand. Markerly did a recent study on Instagram and after analyzing 800,000 users showed that the ROI on partnerships with "micro-influencers" (roughly 5,000 to 100,000 followers) outperformed that of a mainstream celebrity. Influencers within the 10,000 to 100,000 followers proved to have the best relevance and reach, proving that "micro-influencers" are a very powerful tool and resource for companies when dealing with social media. There are also what's considered a "mid-level influencer" which falls into the 100,000 to 1 million followers range and lastly, a "macro-influencer" which has 1 million+ followers. Having the larger number of followers could be impressive when trying to land high-dollar sponsorships, but as shown in the research, is not necessarily the biggest key when it comes to influence.

I would argue to say the last and most important quality is trust, as people are trusting influencer recommendations more so than the brand itself. An influencer can be anyone – a blogger, a celebrity, a YouTube sensation, enthusiast, activist, or industry expert – so long as they have established their credibility through consistency of their message. The target audience needs to trust and value the influencers opinion on a product or topic. Studies have shown that millennials tend to lean toward online celebrities while those aged 45 and older sway more towards traditional celebrities. And why is this? As the trend of influencers has grown, consumers are becoming empowered in their purchasing and incredibly savvy when spotting a sponsored promotion. Which makes sense. Influencer marketing is growing in popularity, so consumers are on the watch for inauthentic posts. Environics Communications published a survey in April of 2017 in which they asked people to rate their trust in sources of information regarding products, services, brands or organizations. Not surprisingly, people came in at the #1 spot through sampling, followed closely by word-of-mouth recommendations. Your followers will know when a post is sponsored, if for no other reason than that is information that must be disclosed, so be selective and choose a partnership or product you believe in 100%. You have gained their trust because they believe you are a real person, just like them, and they also believe in the content that *you* have created. When presented with something that is 'canned' or 'scripted,' it should be such a natural fit with your personal brand that it never comes across that way. If you do not truly believe in a product but convince your followers to buy into it, they are going to feel conned. Losing a follower's long-term trust, loyalty and support for a short-term gain are not worth damaging all the hard work you have put in building your reputation and credibility.

When you think about these three things combined, you can take a look at the following and the engagement level. Having a massive following could be viewed as less powerful. If the followers are disengaged the message becomes diluted and less impactful. On the flip side, a smaller following in a very specific niche market with actively engaged consumers could be so small that the reach is not enough to successfully penetrate the market in terms of sales. Everything with social media is fluid, just like the trends. What works today may not work tomorrow, so you have to truly be not only *the* expert in your area of interest but continue to stay sharp on what trends are working and why.

Businesses want to collaborate with influencers to increase awareness or drive sales – or, ideally, *both*. The most traditional way to utilize an influencer is to have them give a product review, but other very common methods that have appeared are contests, giveaways, discount codes, and testimonies. Influencers will then share across their social channel(s) to execute the campaign and are then generally compensated with samples or money.

Influencers had evolved greatly from the initial launch back in the late 1800s when companies were utilizing celebrities and characters to encompass and promote their brands. Think about it. Coca-Cola utilized Santa Claus in their ads dating all the way back to the 1920s before really taking off in the 1930s. They strategically brought joy and happiness into all of their campaigns by shifting the image of a regular man dressed up as Santa, to a jolly, plump, white-bearded fellow who *was* Santa. He became relatable to adults and children, and Coke took full advantage of the emotional connection people have with him. The Marlboro Man, easily considered one of the most memorable brand images, became recognized as America embodied in one masculine cowboy, shifting Marlboro from their feminine image and shooting them to the top of the list for best-selling cigarettes. Dos Equis, anyone? We all want to hang out with the most interesting man in the world. Needless to say, influencers have been around for a while, but in recent years have made the transition from historically traditional marketing to saturating social media platforms. And why is that? Consumers have not only changed in the way they think through the buying process but we also now have tools such as the live video and real-time response capabilities that have enhanced the user experience tremendously. Influencers and consumers are no longer confined to their home and desktop computer. Many are accessing social media from a laptop and on the go from their mobile phones. As discussed earlier, consumers want things that are relevant and authentic without the lag time so it makes sense that marketing has moved to where it most makes sense – the places people are accessing any time of the day, no matter where they may be.

Budgets can vary greatly depending on the goal of the campaign and end results, but in the upward ROI trend, the need for influencers is certainly not dwindling. Social media is buzzing all day, every day, so the days of being able to succeed 100% organically are long behind us.

Chapter 3
Top Influencers

It is no longer a question of *if* marketing via social media works, but a question of how detrimental is it to your business if you are not doing it. Social media platforms are powerful tools, and they've got the analytics to back it up. Millions of ideas, suggestions, opinions, and just day-to-day moments are shared daily on social media. Loving someone's shirt? Or maybe you are really interested in where they got their new gym bag. Chances are they can tell you exactly how they found it and give you a link to purchase it via social media.

Being an influencer can be a very lucrative job, but it's exactly that – a job. It takes time, and hard work, but very well could lead to your dream career and lifestyle. According to Forbes, the 30 top players – who have built their fame from the ground up and were *not* previously established celebrities – in the social media influencer arena have a combined 250 million followers and individually some of them have an Instagram audience larger than the population of New York City. Furthermore, some of them can get paid as much as $300,000 *per* YouTube video. Not surprisingly, 24 of the 30 are women, and of the 30, most are millennials spanning categories such as Home, Fitness, Beauty, Travel, Food, Tech & Business. As stated by eConsultancy, just under 60% of fashion and beauty brands are already utilizing an influencer marketing strategy, and 21% plan to invest in one over the next 12 months. Click-to-buy has drastically improved over recent years, specifically on platforms like Pinterest and Instagram.

Reigning at the top of the Beauty category is 27-year old Zoe Sugg. She began her career 8 years ago as a teenager broadcasting from the bedroom. She makes millions by making YouTube makeup tutorials and is followed by #2 Ipsy subscription box founder, Michelle Phan, and #3 Huda Kattan, Instagram sensation. In March Sugg, better known to fans online as "Zoelle," posted a video tutorial for gold eyes and berry lips. She states in the very beginning that she is "no expert," but fans love her personable delivery and upbeat charm. She relates to the general public in that she recommends $4 drugstore product as often as high-end retailers. Zoe has also allowed fans insight into her personal life by adding another channel, MoreZoella, that has racked up over 4.5 million subscribers. This was a very smart move for Sugg, considering how saturated the beauty industry has become with influencers since she first launched her YouTube channel back in 2009. She relates to her audience on an interest and personal level, and that is apparent in her audience numbers and engagement. Sugg began and still rules predominantly as a YouTube sensation, but has also branched into a career as a novelist and in 2014 had her name put on a beauty line.

Ever heard of #bbg or 'Sweat with Kayla'? With summer here, I have no doubts you've seen one, if not both, a time or two over the last couple of months. Meet Kayla Itsines, an Australian multimillionaire who got her start as a teenager via Facebook and Instagram, and as of March 2017, the #bbg and related hashtags had been used in over 10 million Instagram posts. Itsines began by posting transformations, healthy recipes and fitness tips and her following grew organically. She has since branched into traveling the U.S. for her Sweat Tour and released a compilation of 200 recipes for healthy eating and lifestyle which became a bestseller. Though she has gained online fame, she still remains relatable to her fans by posting things such as, "You are good enough, smart enough, beautiful enough and strong enough," to her 11.4 million followers.

Grace Bonney got her start fresh out of college in 2004 when she launched her interiors and DIY blog Design*Sponge. She freelanced in photography but noticed that her blog was consistently the best performer. This was when the light went off, and she decided to make that her primary focus. Bonney lands in the #1 spot on Forbes' Home category and rightfully so. Her influence boasts 584,000+ followers on Twitter, 847,000+ on Instagram, 300,000+ on Pinterest, and 327,000+ on Facebook. Not only that, her blog has a *daily* readership totaling over 75,000 as well as 150,000 RSS readers. Last year, she published her second book which quickly became *New York Times*-bestselling compendium 'In the Company of Women', that includes interviews and portraits of over 100 creative women ranging from bakers to tattoo artists and a wide variety in-between. The blog remains independently owned and operated by Bonney, which allows her the liberty to discuss any topic she desires and not shy away from typically taboo politics or issues and that has had a tremendous impact in how she remains relevant with her subscribers. Her most popular post of all time was in 2013 on her experience of coming out. Bonney doesn't regurgitate her content across all of her platforms. Her readers are loyal, and she and her team are careful to make the distinction between each outlet of communities, which is why she is very particular about her choices of partnerships. Currently, her biggest collaboration is with Ann Taylor, but she has worked with giant retailers such as 3M, West Elm, and Mrs. Meyers.

Though a lot of original social media influencers got their start on YouTube, we see an uprising of stars on other platforms. Instagram has over 700 million monthly users, placing it well ahead of Twitter (more than double), Snapchat, and Pinterest, so it really shouldn't come as a surprise this is where influencers are migrating to. They have experienced tremendous growth since their launch in October of 2010. Don't believe me? It took Instagram 28 months to hit their first 100 million users, another 13 months to add an additional 100 million, and 9 more months to reach 300 million. From there, the gaps are steadily closing. They consistently added 100 million users for the next two 9-month periods so by June of 2016 they were at 500 million. A mere 6 months later they landed at 600 million, and within 4 months of that they completed another milestone and crossed the threshold for 700 million users. Instagram users not only actively *seek* content from their favorite brands or influencers; they want to consume it! Instagram's user base is growing faster than any other social media platform, and eMarketer predicts they will add an additional 26.9 million users between 2016 and 2020. It won't be long before Instagram joins Facebook in the 'billion-user club' as they continue to gain more of the market from their competitors.

Instagram is continuing to keep up with its growing popularity with its user-friendly functionalities. They have even gone a step beyond and focused their efforts on building products specifically to those who have weak connectivity. Again, they are continuously improving on the major thing that people want – to be connected with one another. While in the application, a quick search will get you the latest information from someone and if they are relevant and credible, they have quickly gained themselves a new follower. Ever improving tools such as the "Explore" page makes this even easier than before and can actually eliminate any real searching on a user's end because it actively suggests posts and accounts to follow that are similar to interests that user has shown via their activity.

Everyone is looking for the newest, latest, hottest, trendiest, most informative or affordable XYZ. The opportunities are endless. For example, @weedhumor is rising in the ranks of Instagram fame with over 2.1M followers and an impressive level of engagement. They focus on delivering one thing and one thing only: relatable humor. Tim Karsliyev founded Daily Dose and has such a large network that one out of four people using Instagram can be reached. Daily Dose was innovative in that it was the first motivational accounts on Instagram and is still one of the largest. Karsliyev believes people have a duty to act and from there, Daily Dose was born. Seb Lester, an English artist, type designer, and calligrapher, quickly gained a massive following for his designs and calligraphic prints. He posts videos of himself hand-drawing famous logos. His first post was in November of 2012, and he has already grown to over 1.1 million followers.

Needless to say, you can find just about any market on Instagram, so before getting started, you need to think through which one you want to influence, and how it is you are going to want your brand presented. You will want to remain consistent in your voice and content. When someone is scrolling through Instagram, it is important that they be able to recognize you or your brand, and this will happen over time with repetitive consistency. Include imagery that is appealing visually and include text that elicits emotion. Creating a connection early on with viewers will be key. You will also want to create a hashtag (or two) that are specific to you. Doing this will dramatically increase views on your page if used correctly in a way that makes sense to your market. Include it in your posts and be sure to monitor it to check if other users have incorporated it. If you share on outlets other than Instagram, be sure to include it there and give users a call to action to follow your Instagram page. If it is catchy, users will begin to use it. The hashtag(s) will need to be somewhat short and easy enough for users to remember, while still relevant to your brand. Do your research and make sure it's not already being used. You will want to build your hashtag(s) from the ground up which will require some work, but this is a much better option than competing against someone who has already established content under the same hashtag.

Chapter 4
How to Grow Your Followers

So, you've got your Instagram account set up, your brand guidelines set, and you are ready to be the next great influencer – now what? You need to grow your followers, but how? With Instagram's explosive growth, there are several methods to doing this, so you will have to determine which is the most relevant or feasible for you, but before you start driving users to your page, is your bio where it needs to be?

Having a solid bio is important for a couple of reasons. The first being that it tells people who you are! It also lets them know what you do and what your personal brand is all about. Consumers are pretty quick to judge. They typically take less than a second to form an opinion once landing on your page. Yes, really, so a strong bio will include your area of expertise and a call-to-action such as, "Follow me for more tips on *fill in the blank*!". Your character limit is pretty small, so massage your message until it's just right. You can also throw in some emojis for an added punch.

When you are just getting your feet wet, you will want to take advantage of the tools provided for you. Instagram Stories have taken off since being introduced last year. More than 100 million users use it daily, so it's kind of a big deal. They're a fun way to engage with your audience and continue to foster a meaningful connection. It gets better. As mentioned in the last chapter, the Explore page is a powerful tool on Instagram and can help boost your followers tremendously. If your content is exceptionally engaging, Instagram will actually *recommend* your story to users with similar interests as yours. Having one of your Stories featured will drive tons of users you hadn't previously interacted with and all organically. Take the time to invest and make your videos interesting. A whopping 65% of all ad impressions on Instagram are videos which make sense due to videos getting a higher engagement rate than static images. That's not to say that all your posts should be videos.

An impressive 40 *billion* photos have been shared on Instagram since its launch in 2010. The most popular filters are Clarendon, Gingham, and Juno/Lark, but you will want to use whichever one best fits your style (or none at all!). Whatever you choose, consistency will be key as well as provide high-quality images. Did you know that 60% of the top brands utilize the same filter for all of their posts? That is pretty interesting to think about, but as we've already established, social media trends are constantly changing, so it really is whatever works best for your brand.

Now that you've got the aesthetic foundation laid, do not neglect your caption. It needs to be – again – engaging. Think about asking your followers a question or actually giving them an action item by telling them to comment. And, as discussed earlier, do not forget your hashtags. In doing some quick research, you can uncover the most popular hashtags used throughout your market to add to your personal brand hashtag. By using them appropriately in your posts, you will increase your chances of reaching the right people who want to hear what you have to say. In fact, according to research published earlier this year by Simply Measured, posts with at least one hashtag see a 12.6% higher engagement rate than those with none. If you are an expert on matte lipstick, it makes sense you would want to somehow incorporate #lipstick in your post. A caption that is well put together with strong hashtags will unveil your posts to a wider range of users. The more visible you are on Instagram, the better your chances are of getting more likes, attaining new followers, and increasing your accounts engagement.

On the topic of hashtags, you should certainly leverage those that are already established. Browse through those that are trending, and when it makes sense, be sure to include those as well. For instance, #selfie or #photooftheday are popular and can be easily fit into your post without seeming awkward or out of place. There are also popular themes that can be used throughout the week such as #TBT or #MotivationMonday. If you are incorporating quotes into your mix, you can also piggyback off of #instaquote or #quoteoftheday. Now that you've covered a wide range, also include hashtags that zero in on your target community. The more specific you are, the narrower your audience becomes, but the more likely you are to be seen by them and generate engagement. When using hashtags, a few are alright to cover your brand, a general, and a targeted segment, but exactly how many to use is hard to nail down. Some say using five or more will typically dilute not only your content but your credibility as well. The last thing you want to do is come across as desperate for followers, rather than knowledgeable in your area of expertise or opinion. Other suggest using between 20-25 (30 being the max that you are actually allowed to use). Obviously, the more hashtags you incorporate, the better your chances are at getting more eyeballs on your account, so I recommend being thoughtful and perfecting the craft of your captions. An alternate option is to put your hashtags as the second comment on your photo. Whatever you decide, tell your story and place your hashtags strategically in a manner that works best for you and your brand. After all, this is a business.

Now that we've covered the basics of the power of the hashtag let's go just a bit further and combine hashtags with Instagram Stories. Instagram just announced the launch of Stories Search, which will allow users to browse stories based off a hashtag topic or geographical search. Tagging your location is one last push you can do to gain a few more views on your page by adding your location to your post or story. Not only can users browse hashtags, but they can also browse locations. TechCrunch just broke the news that Instagram is actively testing Location Stories to feature on the Explore page, which has since been confirmed by Instagram. This is still *very* new, so you want to take advantage of this ASAP to better your chances of actually being featured in the spotlight by Instagram.

Once you have perfected a post that satisfies your standards (number of likes, engagement in the comments), it is not a bad idea to recycle the content at a later date. I mean, why reinvent the wheel? If you had a post that performed outstandingly, make a note of it to reincorporate at a later date. It probably goes without saying you won't want to post the *exact* same thing, but there's nothing wrong with having a blast from the past. Plus, it will be new to followers you have gained since originally posting. Refresh the post enough so that it is not redundant to your long-time followers, or opt to keep it generally the same and *clearly* explain it is a throwback, so your new followers have context and your more senior followers have a chance to pleasantly reminisce, as opposed to thinking you are trying to pull a fast one and are – *gasp* – out of fresh content.

So now that we have the content figured out, how often should we share it? In a study conducted by Forrester, 11.8 million user interactions on posts made by 249 branded profiles were analyzed to find that top brands are posting on average 4.9 times per week. Adjust your strategy to focus on the timing and frequency of your posts. Utilize insights that will tell you the time and day your posts get the most engagement and take advantage. Instagram provides a plethora of insights all at your fingertips giving you access to your followers' gender, location, age, and most importantly when they're most active. In a recent poll of over 50% of social media managers, it was reported the best time to post for them was between 7 and 9pm. Another study showed a prime time for posting is at 5pm or 2am. Another article has stated Wednesdays specifically. That being said, remember every niche and target audience is unique, so it might take some research on the front end and a bit of work planning, but well worth it since posting, and scheduling tools, is available to you at no cost. For instance, if you are targeting a consumer it is likely that your chances of catching them during non-work hours or a weekend are higher. On the other hand, if you are targeting businesses, it could be more beneficial to be active during the typical work week. You should also be aware of time zones. If you want to gain followers on the west coast but you are located on the east coast, chances are it would not make sense to post right when you are starting your day. Rather, you should wait until they are starting theirs. Knowing your audience and when they are online is especially important since the change of Instagram's algorithm moving away from chronological to giving priority to the posts with the most engagement. Again, consumers want relevancy and Instagram is leading the way in providing this. Essentially, if you do your homework, you will reap what you sow. Posting at a peak time will lead to increased engagement, and increased engagement will lead to more visibility, which will lead to – you guessed it – increased engagement and more followers. Plan to have a large enough library of content that you can implement your findings from your research while also allowing yourself to experiment with your posts. Ultimately, you want to finesse a schedule where you see the most return.

Now that you've got your page in motion, do you know what else is happening in your market? Knowing your competition and siphoning their audience is another common tactic available on Instagram. When you go to your competition's page, you can view their followers. From there, you can engage with their audience by following, liking or commenting on their followers' posts. According to studies done by Shopify, following will produce a 14% followback rate. A follow combined with a like will increase that number to 22%, and a follow + like + comment will garner a 34% followback. Of course, you can always expand beyond this list. Searching Instagram for your target audience is fairly simple. You can browse hashtags and other popular users or photos. Be sure that if you are going to invest the time and effort in doing this, you really make the most of it and truly engage. Put thought behind which photos you choose to like and make your comments thoughtful. It is pretty easy to weed through comments that are being posted for quantity rather than those that are actually trying to make a real connection. Another tip to this method is to try and be the last person to comment on the photo. If you were viewing an Instagram photo and the last comment was interesting, chances are you would likely check out that account, right? Utilize your emojis when appropriate and be unique while staying true to your brand and voice. Stand out. Get noticed.

Lastly, if you are willing to invest a little bit of money, this is a very easy way to grow your followers. And we're not talking about purchasing followers. Seriously, do not do that. You might increase your number of followers, but you will not receive engagement which, as we know, is what makes the world of Instagram go 'round. You *can*, however, boost your own posts to make them more visible without losing your integrity. Your account will need to be a Business Account rather than a personal, so keep that in mind. If that's not the route you want to take, you can also lean into other influencers, and with the right persuasion, for low to minimal cost or better yet, for *free*. Sounds a bit contradicting, but it's not. Much like sponsors, there is a pool (or an ocean depending on your niche) of other influencers who could actually *compliment* your personal brand rather than compete with it. If you have a connection which already has a well-established audience in the same market as you or something relatable, lean into them to give you a quick mention on their page. If you do not personally know anyone, start making connections by building a relationship exactly the same way you would with your audience. Say for instance you are really into healthy foods. There are so many avenues you could explore to begin searching for a partnership. You could branch into the fitness category, or you could even take a look at home goods and interior designers for the plates, bowls, etc. You want the connection to be unique, and who knows – you might actually surprise them, in turn, peaking their interest. Follow their page and get to know them. Remember, people still hold the emotional connection in high regard, so you need to respect that. Just as you want your engagement level of your followers up and meaningful, so do they. Make sure their voice aligns with how you would like yourself to be represented and speak up. Like their photos and leave thoughtful comments. Nurture the relationship before initiating the request for the shoutout so when it comes a time, they already know who you are. You will want someone who has the same ballpark figure of followers as you do because otherwise, it's unlikely you will bring much value in their eyes to the relationship. Case and point: if you've got 10,000 followers you probably wouldn't want to spend much time listening to someone asking for a shoutout when they only have 50.

Craft your request thoughtfully to ask users if they'd be interested in a shoutout. Look at their bio to see if they have contact information (i.e., an email address) listed, but if not then opt for an Instagram Direct private message. Be conscious that since the launch of this feature, spam has increased. Make sure your message sounds genuine and comes across as a real human rather than a robot. After your best efforts, if the user chooses not to engage with you, send a follow-up message. If they still do not respond to your inquiry, remember to always be polite and thank them anyway. Compliment them on their work and remain actively engaged with their account to show them you are serious. After all, this should have been someone you were genuinely interested in, right? And you never know. They could always change their mind, or come to you down the road. Who you know can be very powerful, so you always want to leave a (positive) lasting impression. A lot of relationships take the time to build, so don't be deterred if people aren't jumping at your requests right off the bat.

Chapter 5
How to Increase Your Engagement

In the previous chapter tips were shared on how to increase your followers, but now that you've got them to your page, how do you engage with them? At this point you're probably thinking 'I get it,' but I cannot stress enough how important this piece of the puzzle really is! Engagement with your followers will be the key to your Instagram success, and, according to bitcatcha, Instagram posts get 58 times more engagement than Facebook and 120 times more engagement than Twitter so you really should be capitalizing on this opportunity.

Alright, so now that you have gotten followers to your page, remember to stay active! It may seem pretty straight forward, but nothing drives followers away more than having nothing to absorb. Be sure that you are giving users enough content to digest, and as mentioned in the last chapter, be sure that you are reciprocating the effort. Comment and like others' photos to keep the conversation going. If they ask you a question or leave a comment, be sure to respond in a timely manner, and as always, be thoughtful in how you engage with them. If you see that they left a powerful comment on your page that is helpful to you when other viewers see it, spend the extra 2-3 curating a response that is just as impressive. Businesses typically lose the edge of the personal touch, which is where you can have a huge advantage over them. Social media is all about human interaction, so that is exactly what people want.

A great way to start increasing engagement is by Regramming. Regramming is when you post another account's photo to your own account (with the proper credit, of course), and is one of the easiest and most effective ways to engage with your audience. As always, be mindful in what you select. You want to look for high-quality content that is consistent with your look and feel and supports your brand. Do you have a follower who is your biggest fan and consistently liking and commenting your photos? Is there another who has a large following themselves? When a fan receives a personal shout-out from you, it will only strengthen their engagement and encourage them to continue on and quite possibly turn into a brand ambassador for you. It shows them you see them, you appreciate them, and you are willing to connect with them! Think about it. If one of your favorite influencers or brands shared your photo, you would get pretty excited about it, right? They would essentially be giving you some very public kudos for an awesome post. Same rules apply to *your* fans. You turn a somewhat emotionless connection into a meaningful one while cross-pollinating your Instagram accounts. In seeing this, other fans will be motivated to submit great content and voila, you yourself have even more great content and supporters.

In Chapter 4 we touched briefly on why your captions are important for getting more views on your content, but we did not really dive into how to make it engaging for your followers. Believe it or not, your photos and videos are great, but captions help tell your story and captivate your audience. A cool picture at the lake? Great, but why is it important? How is it different than all the other lake pictures? Put some thought into it because, after all, it's your story and that should be something you want the world to care about hearing. Slip in interesting, but relevant, hashtags and emojis to add another layer of interest. After all of that, if you're finding yourself in a lull for excitement, consider asking your followers a question. A simple question such as, "What's your favorite memory from the lake?" can easily get the conversation started. When your followers start engaging, remember to engage back! This may sound simple, but it's actually a common mistake. Just like users get excited about seeing their content shared, they will get excited to personally hear from you. When your followers start to increase this will begin to be an investment of your time, but remember the value that it brings. Be strategic in blocking time after a post so that you are able to be thoughtful in your responses. Thank those for leaving positive comments and give genuine, personable answers to those who ask questions. After all, they value your opinion which is why they follow you! Do not be afraid to show your personality in your comments; it's what makes you unique. For instance, say you were browsing your favorite brand's page. They are a company who travel and post pictures everywhere they go with their dog. Suppose you left a comment such as, "your dog looks so happy!" and the brand responds with, "Thank you, she was! (emoji, emoji, emoji)". Now, while it's pretty cool they took the time to respond to you individually, how much more of an impact would it leave on your if they said something more thoughtful like "thank you! We noticed she looks a lot like the dog in your photos. Goldendoodle?". WOW. Imagine the difference just a few minutes can make! Now those are all positive and fun, but unfortunately, a time will come where you will receive negative comments. When this happens, the same thoughtfulness should be applied. It's the internet, so it's bound to happen where someone disagrees with you and wants to make it known. And that's ok. Pay attention to those as well. They could give insight into a perspective maybe you hadn't yet thought about and, if an appropriate response is crafted, you could very well turn their mindset around and gain a new fan. Look at every comment as an opportunity and make the most of each one. Say you are raving about a new restaurant you just tried and someone comments how much they hate it and how awful their experience was. Rather than ignore the comment and move on, ask them what their favorite place is and why. Telling them, you are always looking for new places to try and showing them you value what they have to say could actually lead to them sending you new places to post about!

Another easy way to break up the norm and drum up engagement on Instagram is through contests. There are several different styles of contests, so it's up to you on which one you lean towards most. The first and simplest type of contest is a like-to-win. Essentially, it's exactly what it sounds like. You will encourage followers to "like" your post and follow you. It takes very little effort on the user's end and you gain yourself new followers. If you are consistent with your contests, it will help build momentum through consistency. Make them fun and exciting, and vary the prize each time you do it for some variety. If you get enough users to engage you're your contest, it might just show up on the Explore page! A very similar method but a step beyond is a comment-to-win promotion. In doing so, it gets your followers involved and can also provide you with some valuable feedback so be meaningful in your directions on what to comment. A slight variation of this is, rather than having them leave a message in the comments, have them tag a friend. This will help you get organic traffic directly to your account. The last most common contest that is rather passive in terms of what it takes to enter is a repost-to-win contest. Having users repost your content allows you to keep control of the message you are sharing as well as the aesthetic piece of it. You will want to have users tag you and/or use the hashtag you created to help keep track of entries. If you want to step up the level of engagement, have users submit their own photos. As mentioned in the beginning of this book, selfies are everywhere on social media. Running a selfie contest with a hashtag gets engagement up and creates a fun sense of competition. Other users will be able to see all the submitted photos, which makes it more interactive. Instruct entrants to tag your account in their submission, which will help get more visibility to your page. The contest is simple, but fun. You can give away an actual prize, or feature the selected winner on your page. Keep the entry rules simple that way followers are more inclined to participate. Having a short entry period will create a sense of urgency, and posting a reminder before the contests ends will get you one final push for last minute entries. Once your follower count is up, you should also consider a contest that requires voting. A contest with voting will motivate contestants to share with friends, family, and other users that they have entered to win your contest which will help raise awareness and drive additional traffic. Keeping track of the voting process will be a task, so be sure to keep the method of entry and rules to a minimum. Now that you have an overview of the most popular Instagram contest styles, choose the one that fits your objectives best. If you are just starting and simply want new followers, a basic approach is the like-to-win. If you have a pretty engaged fan base and would like to tap into their connections, the tag-a-friend method is appropriate. Do your homework and see what your competition is doing. Take note of what they do well, and be sure to blow what they do not do well out of the water. Remember, be sure to remain loyal to who you are and unique. After all, you aren't just competing with other influencers. You are also competing with companies. In addition to checking out your competitors, you can also search more general hashtags like #contest or #giveaway for additional ideas (it is also a good idea to include these when you launch your promotion so others will come across it). If you are having users submit their own content, it would be a good idea to create a theme. That way, when others come across your hashtag, the content submitted will feel cohesive with each other, but also with your brand. Your prize will be a huge factor in your engagement. Know your audience and what appeals to them. Are they more interested in their own moment of fame? Or would a product or gift card make more sense? You want to get your target audience excited and motivated to participate. Be sure your prize makes sense and is relevant. Are you wanting to be an influencer in the music industry? Maybe you could consider giving away a pair of tickets for your favorite up-and-coming band. Or, perhaps there is a new brand of headphones launching that you are just in love with and think your followers would be too! The amount of effort required to enter should be reflected in the prize. Get creative. You want your contest to be exciting and stand out from the rest. Once you have all the details ironed out, you will want to bring it all together with visually appealing graphics. You will want one that announces the contest with clear and precise instructions on how to enter and what they will win. You will also want a reminder graphic to post as the contest begins to come to an end. Lastly, you will want an exciting graphic to announce the winner. You could also opt for a video, based off what your audience responds best to. Lastly, you always have the option to cross-promote on other social media platforms. Once the winner is selected, be sure to notify them with clear instructions on how to claim their prize (if necessary), and also thank all those who participated. This is an opportune time to give a sneak peek of any future promotions that are on the horizon. Instagram does have some promotion guidelines, essentially stating the following:

1. You are responsible for the operation and promotion including rules, terms and eligibility requirements, compliance with rules and regulations regarding prizes

2. You cannot encourage users to inaccurately tag (if they aren't in the photo, do not instruct them to tag themselves)

3. Promotions must include a complete release of Instagram by each participant and acknowledgement that the contest has no affiliation (administered, sponsored, endorsed, associated, etc.) with Instagram

4. Instagram cannot assist in any way regarding advisement of consent

5. If you do use Instagram to administer your promotion, you are doing so at your own risk

You can find more information on all of the above guidelines at Instagram's Help Center.

As stated earlier, Regramming can be a pretty cool thing so make sure you are covering your bases to have your own content regrammed by properly tagging your photos. Love a new fitness pre-workout that just hit the market? Or what about these awesome workout gloves that are not only trendy but comfortable? Tag the company! If it's a product that just launched, they might find your post intriguing enough that they repost it to their page and *boom* – you've got a new channel of people being directed your way.

Regardless of which route you choose to take, be sure your posts always include a call-to-action. Sure, a like is great, but a follow, and a comment is even better. Try asking them questions to get the conversation flowing. Ask their opinion on a topic, or what their favorite of something is and why. If you can encourage the conversation and make it easy for them to engage, you are likely to see more of it. Checking in regularly with your followers on *their* pages will also help drive more engagement on *your* page. If someone sees an interesting comment you left and found it meaningful, they are going to make their way over to your page. The generic "nice (emoji)" will instantly be overlooked compared to something like, "I love your thoughts on ABC. I had never thought of it from that angle. When did you first get interested in it? I typically utilize 123 because 456, but would love to hear more about why you choose this method".

Chapter 6
How to Get Paid Sponsorships

As we have already stated, Instagram can provide you the potential to make some serious cash, but you have to be willing to put in the work. Starting out, it will take time, effort, and commitment, but our goal is to get you to at least $1,000 per month. According to Adweek, most marketers in 2016 spent between $25,000 and $50,000 per influencer marketing program, and that number was expected to double in 2017.

Being an influencer has major perks. You create your own content, work with the brands you so choose to, all while on your own terms and getting paid! So, you have done what you need to do in terms of getting your followers to your page and getting engagement up. Now what? Money.

Social media has become such an ingrained part of everyday life we forget just how new it really is. In a report conducted by The Telegraph, the average person maintains at *least* 5 social media accounts, spending about 20 minutes on average per account per day. This totals out to just shy of two hours *daily*. Though the market may seem saturated, it is still very feasible to begin your journey today towards becoming the next top influencer. There is an endless pool of users who are hungry for content, and there are tons of businesses out there who are still new to Instagram or, quite frankly, do not quite grasp the concept of it. They may get it with no uncertainty but have the time to invest into it. Whatever it may be, there are a few things that are certain. Brands will always want their products promoted. They will always want people talking about their products in the best light, and they will always want to drive more sales. The other thing is without influencers (aka content creators), social media would be a dead zone. The main reason a platform exits the market is that the top influencers have exited the platform. Know your value, especially in your specific arena.

At this point in the game, you should have completed an extensive amount of research. You should have a clear understanding of your personal brand, your market, and who your target audience is. You should have your rhythm down to a science on how and when you present yourself. While you have been getting to know your competition, it is equally important to have a pipeline of those who would be a good fit for a partnership. It needs to make as much sense to them and as much, if not more, than it would to you and be mutually beneficial.

It's hard to say exactly where you should start without knowing what your expertise is, but a good general starting point is to think about the tools that you use every single day. If you are a photographer dominating the scene on your platform or even in your geographical area, think about what cameras you use. Is there a local shop that would make sense as a potential sponsor? What about the bags you carry your equipment in? Is there one that is your personal preference that you could rave about without sponsorship, so it comes naturally? Is there a local venue that you find yourself at repeatedly? Or are you constantly on the go for destination weddings? Do you count on a local bank you to fund your traveling or business expenses? If any of these were answered with 'yes,' they are very viable options for sponsorships, and you should consider approaching them. All of them. Why? Because you are an expert in your field and touch all of these avenues consistently. And the best part? Not a single one of them compete with one another. Not all of your best partnerships will be the most obvious so be sure to fully open your mind to all options that would make sense.

Now that you have a list of prospect sponsorship opportunities, you need to make sure you have the most impactful approach. When making the initial contact with potential sponsors, you need to make a strong connection right off the bat. You will need to make sure you are conversing with the right person. Otherwise, you are wasting time. A good place to start is typically the marketing department (if it's a larger corporation), or scan the company website and their 'About Us' to see if they have employee profiles posted. Doing your homework will be a great investment of time, and will be clear to the potential sponsor. Connecting in person is always ideal, but you have to start somewhere so if you are not able to meet face-to-face, opt for a phone call rather than email, so you stand out and are more memorable. Emails are easy to ignore, and often times get filtered out quickly. Be yourself and have a compelling story, but also back it up with the facts of your industry. In having a strong story, you will create an emotional connection that sets you apart from other influencers. Be sure that you are clear about what it is you do. Why is it helpful for them to have you in their corner? What is it that you bring to the table? Do not make someone guess (or even come close to having to guess) about why it is you are someone they need on their team. If you have hard facts and figures, put them out there. Businesses love numbers. If you can get them in front of 150,000 sets of eyeballs, tell them that! There is power in quantitative numbers. The more you can show them a strong collection of numbers (think followers, click-through rates if you have them, or conversions on previous collaborations or sponsorships), the better your case will be. On the topic of numbers, do not sell yourself short when asking for your pay. After all, this is your income. When you're dealing with businesses, don't be afraid to ask for what you really want. Have confidence in your value. Also, if you see the potential for multiple opportunities, ask for a longer partnership rather than a one-time deal. This will save you time and effort from having one source as opposed to having a handful for the same amount. Being organized with your communication and follow-up is imperative.

In addition to the obvious perks listed above, there are several more depending on what your goal is. We talked quite a bit about how to improve your engagement, and one of the ways is to hold a contest. Once you land a sponsorship, take advantage of this opportunity. Who you're partnering with should be a company that you have an interest in, so try and aim for at least one where you wouldn't be able to provide the product as a giveaway otherwise. Make it special for your audience since it is something you couldn't do without the sponsor. And, if you play your cards correctly, you can probably get more than just the product to give as a prize. You can likely get the product for you to keep and review, and monetary compensation for highlighting the brand in a positive light.

Once you have a foundation and feel confident in your approach, do not be hesitant or afraid to go for bigger sponsors. Even if the brand already has a large following, find a way to show them what value you could bring them. This will give you a chance to tap into their followers and gain yourself credibility with your fans. This will also help you build your portfolio of work and attract other large sponsors.

When doing your researching for prospective sponsors, you want to be well versed in exactly it is who you are approaching. There are sponsorships out there, but you will also be crossing paths will several affiliates. While they do have the potential to be lucrative as well, they are not a guaranteed amount of money whereas with a sponsorship you will receive a flat rate. Affiliate marketing is essentially an agreement in where you, the influencer, get a commission for sales generated from your traffic. This is where knowing the difference is important, depending on which type of market is your niche. For instance, if you are in the beauty market, that can be, depending on what your focus is, a pretty broad range of people so affiliate marketing could be a feasible route. On the flip side, if you work in a very specific market with a small audience, you may see fewer conversions solely for the fact there is less of a market to penetrate. This is where sponsorships could become very beneficial, especially if you know what is happening in the business, in that if you own a small market, they could be willing to pay more for your dominance. A report from The Economist in October of 2016 proved that endorsements on social media are a rapidly growing business and quite lucrative to boot. According to Captiv8, in January of 2016 over 200,000 posts on Instagram had been tagged with #ad, #sp, or #sponsored. Oh, did I mention that was per *month*? They suggested the below breakdown of averages:

- 100k – 500k followers: $5,000/post

- 500k – 1M followers: $10,000/post

- 1M – 3M followers: $50,0000/post

- 3M – 7M followers: $75,000/post

- over 7M follower: $150,000/post

Starting out as a micro-influencer, you will want to be practical (and realistic) and start smaller (somewhere in the $100-500 range for Instagram posts). According to Shopify, in a survey of 5,000 influencers, around 42% said that they charge within the $200-400 range per post. By no means do you want to sell yourself short, but you want to be fair to your potential sponsors and leave a good impression. In doing so, you will be setting yourself up for success for future opportunities to work together again, or gaining solid testimonies to include in your presentation when you go to pitch to other sponsors. Social media offers businesses a unique way to speak to millennials in the way they want to consume information. Influencers are able to bridge the gap and connect with their audience in a way that traditional marketing cannot. Remember back in Chapter 1 when we discussed women as a trend in social media, specifically, the millennial mom? Weber Shandwick uncovered that 42% of these moms do not feel that advertisers understand them. If you are a millennial mom, this could be a *huge* opportunity for you to make some serious cash. If you are not, or if you are but that isn't really your passion, you should still be connecting with brands who want to connect with your followers, which makes you the perfect fit. You should connect so well with the people they want to target because *you* are *their* target! This is powerful and should certainly be used in negotiations.

Once you become a well-known influencer, chances are the brands will seek you out, but until then if you are unsure about which brands to target for sponsorships, there are several tools available to you to get you started. Assuming you are just starting out with a smaller following, here are some recommendations to research:

- Crowdtap: this company's model is set up as a rewards system (think product samples, gift cards, etc.) with major players like McDonald's, Folgers, Neutrogena, and Aveeno. While you won't see monetary compensation, this is a *great* resume builder that will stand out to other sponsors.

- indaHash: with this company, you do get paid. You will sign up with them and from there can view available sponsorships. They utilize an algorithm that determines your followers' engagement, and from there, your rate is determined as well as which jobs you are able to see.

- Fohr Card: if you have other channels in addition to Instagram, this could be a great option. This company allows you to connect all your social media platforms to essentially create and influencer sheet with all your stats. You can also access a list of brands and what they are looking for so you can take the initiative to reach out as well.

- Grapevine: once you hit 5,000 followers, you can join this network and gain access to their Brand Sponsorship Marketplace. From there you can submit proposals or receive proposals from brands that are interested in collaborating.

- TapInfluence: similar to indaHash, this resource takes the guesswork out of aligning yourself with appropriate brands. You will create a profile that describes yourself and gives an overview of the nature of your content, and you will be presented to brands that might be a good fit.

These are just a few, but the list goes on and on which makes it easy for you to have tons of opportunities right at your fingertips. If you really want to succeed and make money from your presence on Instagram and are willing to put in the work, it is 100% possible to succeed and be well on your way. The numbers and statistics provided to you prove that Instagram is growing and the world of influencers is not going anywhere anytime soon. To conclude, let's highlight the top 5 key steps to help you in your success to monetizing your Instagram account:

1. Determine what it is you want to establish yourself as a thought leader on. It needs to be something that you are extremely passionate about. Remember, you will be pushing out content on this day, after day, after day. It needs to be a topic that truly excites you and is something you believe in. You will be required to do some homework. Research the market including target audience, competition, and successful brands. It is important to have an understanding of what they are doing, and what they are not doing. Also, you need to be aware of what they do well and what areas they could improve on. Being in tune with these things will only help you with your personal brand and building it to be as strong as possible. Have a clear roadmap of your goals and what you want to accomplish. Keep your content consistent. You want your followers to be able to recognize your work among the masses.

2. Stay sharp on social media trends and know what is happening in the market. The top trends for 2017 are: messaging, videos, augmented reality, and the improvement of business tools. You need to be aware of what is working, or what is not working, and how it relates

to your followers. You should lean into trends as often as possible, and be sure that things are making sense with the arena you are playing in. Always be aware of what your competition is doing but remain true to yourself and your brand. You want to provide authentic content that is natural because it is *you*.

3. Bring top-notch quality content to the table every single day. Your photos should be visually interesting and appealing to your audience. Make sure that you are covering all bases including imagery, captions, and hashtags. Each of these is something you should be taking advantage of, and you should be giving each one maximum effort and thought. Utilize your ability to get creative and be unique in your caption. Be sure to include hashtags that are specific to your brand and niche, but also some that are more generic that will help you keep a larger reach at all times.

4. Put in the effort to have a strong following and continuously keep it growing. Maintain fresh and thought-provoking content and be creative in methods of uncovering new users. Always keep engagement top-of-mind. Remember that Instagram runs off engagement levels, so be diligent in putting in the effort to make a connection with your audience. You want them to feel the emotional connection to you and always have them coming back for me. Keep it fun. Keep it authentic. Keep it true to *you*.

5. Until the sponsorships come to you, don't hesitate to go after them. Be realistic in your conquests, but also confident in your accomplishments. Be selective, and be strategic with your prospects, and most importantly be persistent and give it time. Make sure that you have a strong community of followers and once your foundation is solid, start getting serious about your business. Remember that $1,000 a month is easily doable, and there is no shortage of funds out there. Brands are looking for influencers just like you, and it's up to you to make the connection and partnership.

Conclusion

Thank you for making it through to the end of this book! I hope it was entertaining and especially informative in providing you with the tools you will need to achieve your goals in becoming the next top influencer of Instagram.

You have been provided with a quick glimpse into the ever-changing world of social media with personal opinions as well as statistics. A brief overview of a handful of current social media influencers has been provided, and you are now armed with the basic tools and knowledge to make your account attractive to potential followers when they land on your page. I have also covered common tips and trips on how to grow your followers, and most importantly what to do once your following has expanded. You are now informed with popular ways on how to *engage* with the audience. Additionally, a basic guideline has been provided on what to think about when considering sponsorships and how to seek out potential sponsors. Helpful ways on how to begin the relationship and recommended methods have been discussed, and you are free to choose whichever works best for you, or you can also tweak any to make your own personal approach. In your next steps, you will immediately want to start thinking about your personal brand and strategy, and from there you can begin your journey as the next up-and-coming Instagram influencer.

I hope you have enjoyed this read!